Sales Force

The Four Most Powerful Social Media
and Sales Tools in the Universe

Maury Rogow

Lightning Press

London

Copyright © 2013 Maury Rogow

Sales Force is an allegorical sales tool, or parody, designed to teach every aspiring entrepreneur how to cultivate an idea and create a successful business. The author and the *Sales Force* are not affiliated in any way with Lucasfilm Ltd., Disney, Salesforce.com, any Star Wars products, including films, books, games, and merchandise. New elements and many lessons have been introduced to help businesses grow in this exciting, yet overwhelming time in digital marketing.

Registration: 1-659631181
COPYRIGHT: TXU 1-774-886
ISBN:
978-1-4675-3616-5
978-1-4675-3617-2
978-1-4675-3618-9

I would like to thank:

The late Kevin Keehn for a business development position in an amazing startup company. His legacy and fun stories live on.

Kevin Gallagher for always being on the side of his sales team fighting for the customer first, his sales team second, and personal desires last.

Kevin Brady for the instilling the importance of being the first one in the office, and being the most organized person in the building.

Donna Sozio for important contributions to the structure of this story.

Jim Sprague, for believing these words hold special lessons for every entrepreneur.

Ann Murray as an editor, and for being wonderful to work with.

Sharon Rogow, Nathan Rogow, Brad Rogow and Jeffery Horovitz for always believing in my wild ideas.

—Maury

TOC

Contents

WE DIDN'T SEE IT COMING	10
THE BULL	14
The Story	19
The Lucky Break	24
Master Quoda	28
Introduction to the Sales Force	32
The Power of the Sales Force	42
The Power of the Dark Side	49
Training Begins...Again	54
Grow Your Business with the Sales Force	64
Getting the Sale	72
Lessons Learned	76
Appendices	80

Foreword

This is the classic "hero's journey" told in parody form. We are all heroes and can achieve great things. No business survives without the creation of the idea, the implementation of the idea, and *sales*.

The lessons here will help you launch a new product and "get the deal."

This parody is meant to entertain, teach, and inspire.

CHAPTER 1

WE DIDN'T SEE IT COMING

SCANNING THE VAST banquet hall in this luxurious Silicon Valley hotel, I watch happy sales teams taking notes with commemorative light pens. Our company has banners emblazoned with our new logo decorating the walls. One executive after another is heralded onstage with applause. The sales teams are enjoying pats on the back and a lavish never-ending seafood buffet. I am particularly enjoying the jumbo crab claws and lobster salad. Feeling on top of my game, I nod to one of my coworkers, as if to say, "Could this get any better?" while wiping a blob of seafood sauce from my chin.

Our company president has an announcement to make. Speaking plainly, he tells the room that he has just hired a new vice president of sales, Don D'Man, who singlehandedly turns startup businesses and new brands into billion-dollar corporations. "He is taking over sales, effective immediately," the president declares. "Please stand up and give him a warm welcome."

My eyes scan the room for the new VP. As Don D'Man slowly approaches the podium, a sudden chill shoots through the room.

He isn't looking jovial. It's as if he isn't part of the celebration at all. There is nothing warm about D'Man. He towers above us and looks like he hasn't missed his daily 20-mile run...ever. His eyes are smart, yet emotionless and black, like a shark's. The expression on his face isn't saying, "Congratulations!" It reads, "Change in command."

He just stands at the front of the room, staring at us. "Intimidating" isn't enough of a word. The applause falters, then stops awkwardly. A fork drops. No one plays with the light pens. The congratulation banners seem out of place. People in the room are wondering what is coming, searching for meaning from anyone with whom they can catch eye contact.

D'Man doesn't want to speak from the podium. He walks right past it. No microphone. He is holding his talking points scribbled onto a tiny white cocktail napkin. He comes straight up to where I stand—so close that I can almost make out the writing.

D'Man begins speaking. "I have three things to say."

We all lean in to listen.

"First. You built a product, not a brand. And, that was last year. Under my watch, you have done nothing."

D'Man stares straight at me. *Me?* Some team members turn to look at me as well. My feet are bouncing...*floor, where are you?*

"Second. If you don't double your sales in the next quarter, I will fire you. I *will* replace you with someone who will."

Double? Replaced?! D'Man finally pulls his gaze away from me, and fixes it on the guy we know to be the weakest link, Neal Fishlyer. Neal gulps. His skin turns an odd shade of green as he nervously rubs his balding head. *Yeah, yeah, you should fire Neal...*

The hit man continues: "Third. If you are a manager and you don't fire your underperformers, I will fire you.

"That is all I have to say."

D'Man crumples his three-note napkin into a ball and drops it. He walks past me and sits down, looking proud of his speech. The room is silent. The free jumbo crab claws and lobster salad don't look appetizing anymore.

I see the last year flash before my eyes. *Wake up 6 a.m., airport. New York, create a sales pitch. Client dinner. Bed at 1 a.m. Wake up at 6, train. Philadelphia, sales pitch. Up again at 6. Washington, partner pitch, prospect dinner, airport, red-eye. New York, contract—Yes! Sales pitch, airport, San Francisco, what time zone am I in? Pitch, write, pitch, press, and pitch.*

My job is to increase demand, develop new business and generate sales. I thought things were so good. Now I am going to get fired?!

All of a sudden, I am in over my head. I need help.

CHAPTER 2

THE BULL

BACK AT THE OFFICE on Monday, I'm not the only one pacing back and forth. I debate talking about the conference with my coworkers. Rumors are already flying, and I need to get the inside scoop, *now*. An idea forms in my mind: Go talk to the guys that know D'Man. Kevin, better known by his alias, "The Bull," and his sidekick, Jake. Jake is young, stays close to the Bull, listens to his every word, and is known for being out for himself.

Both Jake and the Bull have been successful working for D'Man before. They are stone-cold sales machines. I need some inside information to create a new strategy, and to save my keester in the process.

I spot them walking out of a meeting. "Can I ask you guys a question?"

Jake doesn't pay any attention, even though I was the top sales person...*last* year. This year, he would rather take my job than help me.

This is D'Man's ideal guy, I think.

But the Bull answers: "Yeah, let's talk on the way to my office." The Bull has been in sales for what seems to me like an eternity. He would never say exactly how long. But he has weathered many corporate storms even though he surely could have retired nicely long ago. This is a guy who loves every aspect of "the deal."

"My numbers may not double up this quarter," I say. "I have three months to make this happen, or I'm out on the street, according to what D'Man said the other night. Is this real, or hot air?"

Leaving us behind as he strides by, Jake shoots back the answer. "He will fire you. Three underperformers were dusted this morning. He fired that weakling Neal on his way out of the sales meeting. D'Man's got nothing to lose and everything to gain."

It is real.

I appeal to the Bull as we continue walking toward his office. "I want to stay," I tell him. "I've worked so hard. What do I do?"

The Bull states, matter-of-factly, "Upgrade your sales system, learn, and do what it takes. This company is going to be sold. Everyone will be wealthy if they are still here in six months. If you miss quota, you'll be fired."

"I don't have time to go to training classes," I say, trying to keep my voice calm. "I'm already putting in fourteen-hour days. I need help, and now..."

The Bull thinks for a second, as if he is sizing up my worth. "Okay, you want me to tell you how D'Man grows sales, and how I do it?"

I shake my head, incredulous and relieved. "Seriously?"

The Bull calmly continues, "Come by my office at five. We'll go over your potential. You're okay, but this is do-or-die time. Maybe I'll learn something too."

* * *

At 5 p.m., I walk into The Bull's office. He is waiting for me. This guy is always prepared and on time.

Looking around his office, I see a side of his personality that I never knew existed. He has space shuttle photos with himself in the foreground, autographed photos of famous astronauts, and movie posters from some of the biggest science fiction films ever made.

The Bull motions for me to take a seat. "You need to upgrade your sales system," he begins. "You've been spoiled. You were doing well, but the market and technology changed. If you cannot pivot and adapt, you will be left behind."

Then the Bull pauses and seems to chuckle slightly to

himself. "Tell me," he asks, "do you think you have what it takes to launch a new product and make the toughest sale?"

I'm not seeing where he is going with this. "You mean, like selling-ice-to-Eskimos tough?"

"Tougher," he says.

"Well," I venture, thinking of some of my stalled marketing efforts. "It would have all the hard-sell elements. A huge idea. Expensive. Tough customers. "

"Exactly," says the Bull. "Selling big solutions. That is why I love sales. You need to have the skills to create new sales anywhere, in any economy. You need the skills of a great Sales Force."

The Bull sinks into his plush executive chair, and starts telling me a story that is as unusual as it is useful. This story makes it clear to me which of my accounts would close and which ones were pipe dreams.

He uses words like "champion," "personal win," "Wiifm," "decision-making process," and "organization charts." I am overwhelmed. I am humbled. My mind reels with the possibilities for using this business growth sales system.

Pieces of information scatter in my mind from past lecture halls and professional training sessions. Finally they come together with their practical applications. The Bull explains how concepts, when put together, are much more than the sum of their parts. He solidifies, into a step-by-step process, ways to improve my marketing, sales, and product launch ability forever.

This is clearly the best sales system I have ever learned.

I am ready to both launch and grow this business. "That story was more useful than my MBA!" is what I will find myself saying, again and again, long after it's over.

The following is the story the Bull tells me.

CHAPTER 3

The Story

IN THE NOT-SO-DISTANT PAST, in a galaxy not so far away, two alien beings, called 'Entrepreneurs', had a brilliant idea they called the "Life Star." These two, named Luck and Solow, felt the Life Star could overcome and combat overpopulation, pollution, traffic congestion, crumbling railroads, and expensive housing. The Life Star was designed to do nothing less than revolutionize the universe.

Now, Luck and Solow were really a dynamic duo. Luck had a knack for being in the right place at the right time, and thus often seemed to meet just the right person to help him at any given moment. Solow was fiercely independent, attempting to do everything better himself, often relying on his good looks and charm to get exactly what he wanted.

So confident were they that the Life Star would be an instant hit throughout the galaxy, Luck and Solow quit their day jobs. They spent the next six months and the rest of their credit card limits completing a prototype, which they thought, once finished, would sell itself and make them rich. After all, their friends and family were really excited about it.

The day arrived. The Life Star shined. It gleamed. It was ready! Admiring their creation, Luck and Solow virtually patted each other on the back. *It's beautiful, it's perfect*, they both thought.

A moment passed between them. They looked at each other with the same question in their eyes.

"How are we going to sell it?" asked Luck.

"We'll do it ourselves," said Solow. "That way we will get to keep all the profits."

"All we need is a website," said Luck, "so we can get the word out."

Their big friend at Cheapwebba.com built them a website for pennies. Needless to say, they did not realize that this was the only portal through which the world could possibly know about their product.

Luck and Solow expected the sales to immediately pour in.

None did.

Instead of the phone ringing, all they heard were crickets.

Two weeks later. Still nothing.

"Now what?" asked Luck.

An idea occurred to Solow: "We'll plan a Life Star launch party at the Intergalactic Tradeshow!" he said, his face beaming.

* * *

They spent almost everything they had and bought a big ad in a newspaper, the *Daily Star*, and went and set up an expensive booth for the show.

Yet no one came to the booth. Not a soul wanted to learn more about the amazing Life Star.

The thing was, they had created no compelling reason for buyers to be curious and no call to action. They hadn't searched potential buyers and partners, nor contacted any of them before the show. Even worse, on their new low-budget website, they were not able to post updates on their event plans, nor get any news out to social sites, nor attract any interested followers.

Now they had lost some serious cash.

* * *

Luck and Solow realized they were in dire straits. They didn't have a sales plan. They had no leads, let alone any sales. Luck and Solow started desperately calling everyone they could think of, leaving eight-minute voicemails waxing on about how great the Life Star was and how it would make everybody rich.

Again, nothing.

Suddenly, the Life Star looked less shiny. Less perfect. It didn't seem to have much of a force at all.

Luck and Solow asked themselves a new question: "How can customers find us?"

"It's easy," said Luck, "they go to the Galactic Wide Web and type in 'SolowandLuckscoolnewLifeStar.com' and *boom!* – it's right there!"

"How many people search for 'Solow-and-Luck's-cool-new-Life-Star'?" asked Solow.

"Actually, I don't know," said Luck.

"Can the website show us?"

"Not this website. It wasn't built with that ability."

"How many people are talking about our cool new product?" asked Solow.

"Well, I have no way to measure that," said Luck, meekly, "but...likely, no one."

Solow wondered out loud: "Websites get millions of visitors with ideas only a fraction as good as the Life Star. How do they get to be popular sites? How do they appear when people search on the web? How do we become a top-ranked website?"

The cell phone rang. Luck and Solow jumped to answer

it. But it was only Universal Bank inquiring about the debt they took on to build the Life Star.

Luck looked at Solow. Now he was more worried than excited. Bills were stacking up and they didn't know how they were going to pay them.

"What now?" asked Luck.

Their website didn't have a video explaining the benefits of their product or the ease of working with Luck and Solow. They realized no one had time to read anymore, and wondered if the Life Star's Galactic Wide Website was doing them any good in its current condition.

Luck called all his family members in a desperate attempt to get in the door...*anywhere.*

Weeks later, the phone rang for the first time. It was Luck's sister Ally, a new recruit at Stellar Corporation.

"Can you come in tomorrow?" she asked. "I can get you three minutes with the executives at their High Council Meeting."

Luck and Solow nearly dropped the phone.

"We will be there!" they whooped.

"Make it good," Ally said, "otherwise, I'll look bad."

Luck and Solow were excited again. They gave the Life Star a good shine and headed off to Stellar Corporation.

"What luck!" said Luck.

"And we did it ourselves," said Solow.

CHAPTER 4

The Lucky Break

LUCK AND SOLOW stood below the twelve members of Stellar Corporation's High Council.

"Introducing...The Life Star!" said Luck.

Excitedly, Solow pulled a gold velvet cover off the Life Star to reveal the prototype.

Luck and Solow waited for the High Council to "ooh" and "aah," but their faces remained long and unimpressed.

The Stellar Corporation leader, D'cision Maker, asked, "Where is your presentation?"

Luck and Solow pointed to the Life Star.

"That's your *product*," corrected D'cision Maker. "I would like to see and hear your presentation about how the Life Star will help us."

Luck and Solow excitedly waxed on about the Life Star's gadgets, gizmos, and cool lasers.

Ally hung her head.

"What will the Life Star specifically do for the needs of the Stellar Corporation?" asked D'cision Maker. "How will the Life Star help the Stellars reach our goals?"

Luck and Solow were perplexed. They searched the room for answers but didn't find any. Besides, how were they supposed to know? Wasn't it Stellar Corporation's job to know how the Life Star would serve their goals?

"Do you know anything about what the Stellar Corporation needs?" asked D'cision Maker.

Luck and Solow shook their heads.

The Stellar Council members yawned as their eyes glazed over.

D'cision Maker's head shook slowly. "Not for us," he said.

* * *

Luck and Solow had made a big mistake. They thought it was up to Stellar Corporation – and all the other corporations in the galaxy – to know why they needed the Life Star and what it would do for them. Even worse, they made their one ally at Stellar Corporation look bad in front of her boss.

As they left, Luck overheard D'cision Maker groaning to the Council – "They had the *worst* sales presentation in the whole universe!" – and reprimanding Ally for wasting the Stellars' time by bringing in someone so unprepared and unprofessional.

"Maybe we should get our old jobs back," said Solow. "This is just too hard."

"I'll get us back in there," said Luck.

A week later, Luck asked Ally for a second chance. He assured her that they had worked on and largely improved their presentation from what it had been before.

But when Ally asked Luck to detail the Life Star's core competency, explain its solution for the market, and send her testimonials and a video presentation. They couldn't. The duo didn't have that information.

Using his charm, Solow asked Ally to coffee. She accepted. At the café, Ally was all business, telling Solow that she wanted to help, as she did see high value in the Life Star. However, she wouldn't risk her reputation until they were ready with a presentation that was professional, visual, and easy to understand. The pitch would have to incorporate complete research on the needs, goals, and desires of Stellar Corporation.

Ally explained: "The Stellars don't recognize the value of the Life Star because you failed to present it in a way that they could understand. First, you have to identify the unique needs of your customer. Then you present your product to them so they see its value and how it solves their problems.

With everything that has been going on in the universe, the Stellars have a lot of problems. You may have the solution, but you must present it correctly."

Ally got up to leave, but not before handing Solow a card. It read, "Quoda: Advanced Sales Force Training for over 700 years," showing an address on a humid swamp planet. "He trains young entrepreneurs to become masters of the 'Sales Force'," she explained.

Luck and Solow weren't thrilled to travel to a soggy planet. But if that was the only way Stellar Corporation would give them a second chance, it was worth it.

CHAPTER 5

Master Quoda

AFTER LUCK and Solow landed on the strange, swampy planet, a short green creature with big hairy ears hobbled towards them. He shook his cane. "The Life Star, huh? Didn't research Stellar Corporation? Didn't understand Stellar Corporation? Didn't listen to Stellar Corporation?"

Master Quoda whacked Luck and Solow on their heads with his cane and motioned for them to follow him into the swamp.

The two of them winced. Yet the whack was painful to their egos, not their heads, and brought them to their senses as they immediately saw that Master Quoda was right: They had not researched, listened, or asked even one question of Stellar Corporation.

Hobbling deep into the swamp, Master Quoda pointed to his big green ears. "Two big ears I have," he said. "Why? To listen. You must ask the right questions, and *listen*. Do not confuse excitement about your product for the Sales Force. The Sales Force is so much more, and it starts with listening to your clients' needs. Only after you discover the needs can you create a consultation that responds in a language they can understand."

Solow and Luck looked at each other as if they had just heard a new language, and they didn't understand.

"That is just the beginning of understanding the Sales Force," Master Quoda continued. "Understand it you must, if you want to overcome your competition. It's a big galaxy. Lots of competition. Some good. Some bad. Some deathly."

Entering a clearing in the middle of the great, murky swamp, Master Quoda instructed: "You must start your training at the beginning, long before you get to a sales meeting." He then motioned to something in the darkness, and a stumpy, round robot wheeled over to join them. The robot, which he introduced as RMG, projected some glowing words into the dark night sky. Luck and Solow, ever the inventors, looked at each other impressed. They had both taken it for a vacuum cleaner, yet the humble robot was actually a sophisticated presentation machine.

As Luck and Solow looked up, they read the steps involved in learning their first lesson:

Luck and Solow excitedly skimmed the list, checking off the steps in their heads as they went. *Testing the market? Yes! After all, their friends and family had been so excited about the Life Star, how could it not be an intergalactic hit? Proper funding for the product, yes again. They put all their credit on the line and built one, didn't they? Protect your assets, absolutely. They had the Life Star locked up at Solow's place.*

Luck and Solow turned and gave each other a big high-five.

"Master Quoda," said Solow impatiently, "you can skip to the next lesson in the Sales Force. The Life Star is already built and ready to deliver."

RMG shivered a bit. Master Quoda rolled his eyes. He knew the difference between initial plans and actual production, which can be littered with unexpected challenges and setbacks. Did they really have the funding for a long enough runway to launch the company?

But Luck and Solow insisted that the first lesson of the Sales Force had been implemented. With a sigh, Master Quoda motioned for RMG to continue.

CHAPTER 6

Introduction To The Sales Force

RELUCTANTLY, the round robot projected the next key lesson into the dark night sky.

Now, this lesson was something Luck and Solow both agreed that they needed to learn. While they were sure that everyone would want the Life Star, they hadn't identified their target customers specifically.

Master Quoda instructed: "To locate your target customers, first you must research your market to understand its failings. By testing the market, even with a simple galactic web landing page, you can identify what your customers want and need. Then you can identify a specific niche market, and become a source of knowledge for those customers. Pay attention, you must.

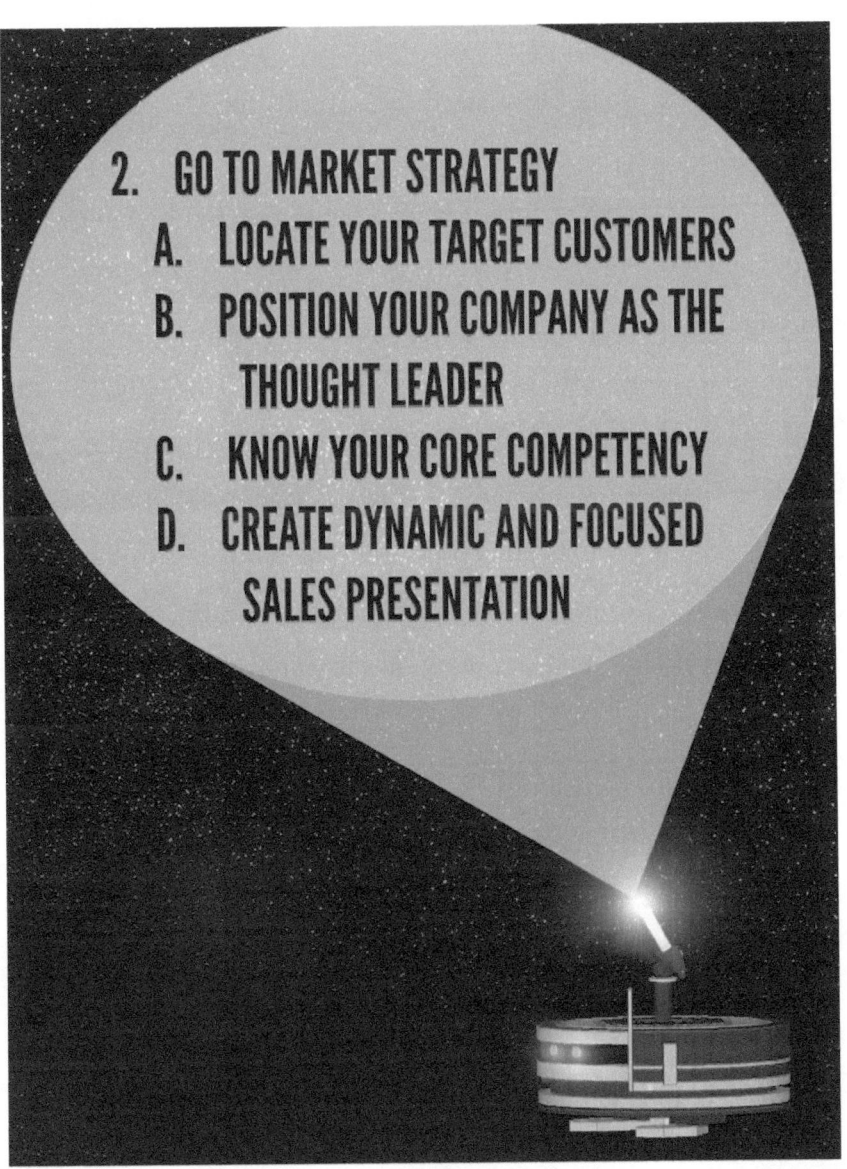

2. GO TO MARKET STRATEGY
   A. LOCATE YOUR TARGET CUSTOMERS
   B. POSITION YOUR COMPANY AS THE THOUGHT LEADER
   C. KNOW YOUR CORE COMPETENCY
   D. CREATE DYNAMIC AND FOCUSED SALES PRESENTATION

"Advertise and research," said Quoda, "until you find an audience with enough demand for your product to become a bestseller. Then you are ready to position your company as the leader in your field. But first, do you know how?"

Luck and Solow shrugged.

"In the early stages, create a basic web landing page and test keywords to drive web traffic to your site. Create a blog and news feed, you must. Speak about what you are passionate about, and invite others to join you. Have others guest write, and speak on the subject you are all passionate about. Post articles, news, expert insight, and your unique thoughts on the subject. Your core audience then has a chance to understand that you are experts in the area and are building a powerful knowledge base. You can now do customer research and collect information on what is needed in the market.

Master Quoda continued: "When your product solves your client's problems, you not only have a sale, but also a lifelong customer. A company that solves customer problems before anyone else is called a thought leader. Thought leaders al-ways have many followers. And thought leaders can be price leaders. As long as you keep listening to your clients' needs, continue adding value, and solve problems with your product, you are on the right path.

"Remember," he said, "you are not selling a product."

Luck and Solow said in unison, "We're not?"

"No," answered Master Quoda, "you are offering your clients a chance to purchase a solution. Offering a solution to specific problems will create value to Stellar Corporation. Remember, in the presence of high value, the question of price disappears. And with high value, your competition disappears as well."

"How do we even get to have prospective buyers, and then have them tell us about their problems?" asked Luck.

Master Quoda was pleased with the question. "Before you know your customer, you must know yourself. First, you must know your core competency. Patience, you must have, in using the full power of the Sales Force." He asked the duo: "What is it that you do better, in a more unique way, or at a higher value than anyone else?"

Luck and Solow searched for an answer.

"With your core competency, you can form an elevator pitch to open the door to an appointment with your target customers. Once you have their full attention, use the power of the Sales Force to present the benefits of the Life Star to your clients. Do you know what an elevator pitch is?" asked Master Quoda.

"Sure," said Solow. "We explain why our product is valuable, within 30 seconds, as if we were on a space elevator with a prospective customer."

"Good you are," replied Master Quoda. "And what is

your elevator pitch?"

The duo stared at the ground, not knowing.

"Hmmm, think you must," advised Master Quoda. "Once you have your elevator pitch, it can be made into a holographic video, which will do much work for you."

"Master, did you say it will work for us, like an employee?" asked Solow.

"Yes, by creating a video that easily explains what you do simply and easily, you can have your product promoted without your being there. It saves you time, money, and increases your chances of success. Properly used, you can have multiple times the impact as you currently have."

"Could this also work for us on client visits, and in trade shows?" asked Luck.

Master Quoda could see that Luck was beginning to think ahead. "Yes, you have one minute to impress your clients, trump your competition, and establish your product as the leader in your niche market. Given all this, you must be prepared with a dynamic and focused sales presentation. Customers make the decision to start working with you – or your competition – instantly. When they notice that you have a professional website with powerful testimonials, press recognition, video explanation, an active and organized call to action, and sales system, they will be positively influenced.

"This is the place to have an expert video produced that

will relay your elevator pitch instantly. Video presentations are always the most effective way to instantly show the value of your product to your customer."

Master Quoda continued: "You must also manage the image of your brand. Therefore, it is important to control exactly how information about your product is broadcast through social networks, the press, blogs, testimonials, and more." Master Quoda paused and said, "Building sales tools will help guide your product promotions."

"What is the best way to do that?" asked Luck intently. "Do you recall, that when you did your first show – and no one came to your booth – you had placed an ad to attract visitors? Where was the STUFF in the ad?"

"Master?"

That was when Master Quoda explained how commercials work, and how people initially pay attention to ads that trigger one of five emotions:

Sensual
Touching
Unexpected
Fearful
Funny

"STUFF, mmmm hmmmm mmm," Quoda giggled. "Yes, one of those elements must be present for people to have interest. In the video, we can use the three most important benefits to your product, and structure a video around these key steps: The Pain, The Dream, The Solution, and The Action. A good video production can highlight the 'pain' of not having what your product delivers, the 'dream' of actually having it, and the 'call to action,' you would like the prospect to take. Very crucial, yes...many years did it take to learn these lessons..."

Luck and Solow sat with eyes and ears wide open, both feeling a bit embarrassed about their low-budget website.

Master Quoda concluded, "A professional website with the right visual presentation is like having an employee who works for you who never sleeps. The Life Star video and website can attract the right customers even while you are on vacation."

"Vacation!" blurted out Luck. "When are we going?"

Whack! Master Quoda knocked some more sense into him. "First you need success in business. Then you go on vacation."

Luck and Solow took heavy breaths. Could they do all this? It seemed monumental. After all, wasn't it enough to create the Life Star? Now they had to become experts in the Galactic Web, and selling, too? Master Quoda could see that the duo needed a break to process all the information they had been given.

Luck and Solow hiked out into the murky swamp to

clear their heads. They weren't in a rush as they were before to meet with prospects unprepared. They discussed how to find a specific niche in the market where the Life Star could dominate, and where their knowledge would be most valued. They decided to build the proper tools to grow sales and work with an expert to help them through the steps they could not do solo.

They thought about their first prospective client and found the basic criteria that would match their target audience. They identified the unique qualities the Life Star had for their target market. Then they tried to "walk a mile" in Stellar Corporation's shoes to understand their unique challenges.

They got online to do research, and found Stellar Corporation's annual report. There were THOUSANDS of pages to sift through. But in the "management discussion" section of the report, Luck and Solow easily found many of the answers they had been seeking. This section specifically detailed Stellar Corporation's shortfalls and goals. Suddenly, the Life Star made more sense when put into the context of solving the challenges of Stellar Corporation and other similar clients in the galaxy.

They also found some top-notch galactic business search websites.[1] Their research had revealed many possible clients across the galaxy with the same needs as Stellar Corporation. Luck and Solow built a plan to contact them directly

---

[1] For a complete list of online tools to grow your business online, see Appendix C: "Web Resources" on page 82.

through social networking. It was an easier, friendlier way to make first contact. They also noticed that by building a large network with a good reputation, they could more easily be introduced to important contacts in a professional manner, rather than attempting to call them 'cold.'

Feeling renewed, Luck and Solow reported back to the clearing and shared their findings with Master Quoda. They also gave their elevator pitch: "The Life Star will decrease costs, drastically increase security, and vastly expand the work area for Stellar Corporation," they told Quoda.

Quoda was quite pleased. It was clear that Luck and Solow were ready for their next lesson.

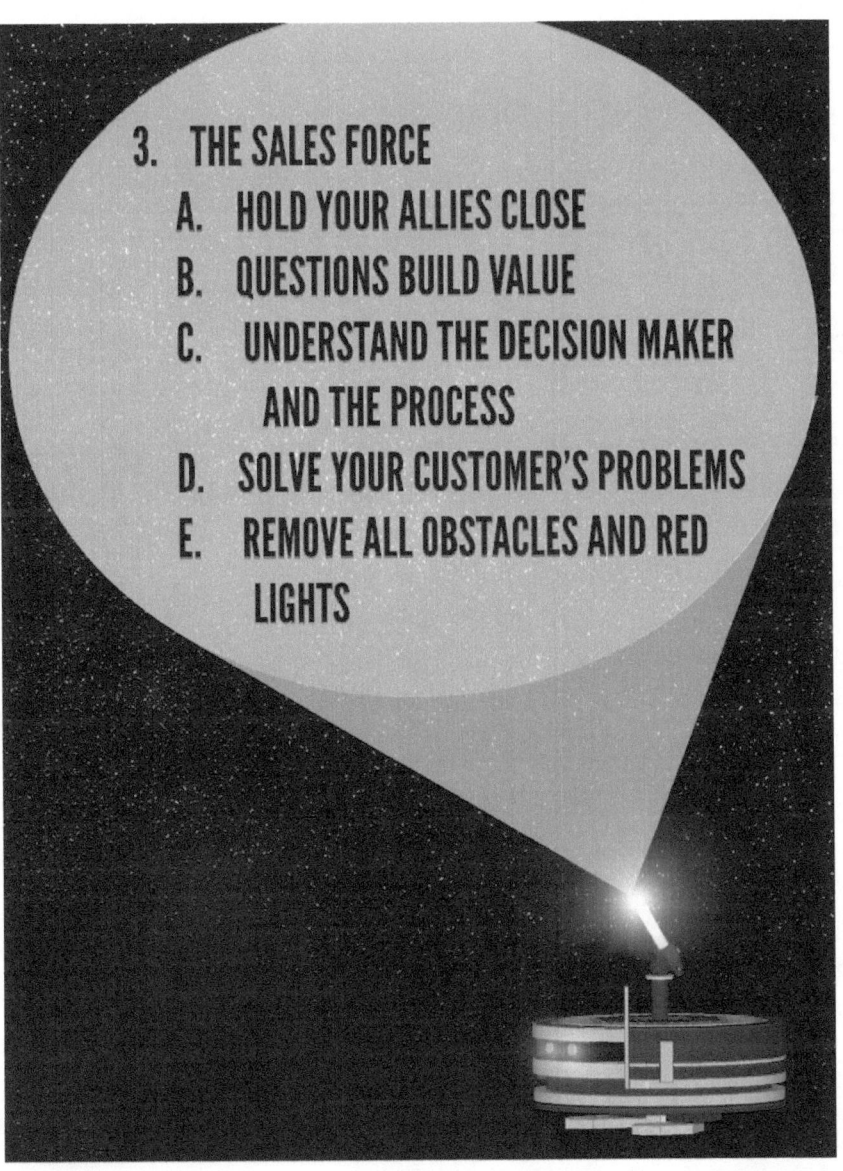

3. THE SALES FORCE
   A. HOLD YOUR ALLIES CLOSE
   B. QUESTIONS BUILD VALUE
   C. UNDERSTAND THE DECISION MAKER AND THE PROCESS
   D. SOLVE YOUR CUSTOMER'S PROBLEMS
   E. REMOVE ALL OBSTACLES AND RED LIGHTS

CHAPTER 7

The Power of the Sales Force

QUODA STARTED with Lesson Three. RMG projected five key points into the dark night sky.

Luck was the first to speak. He understood immediately that Ally was their champion at Stellar Corporation. She was the one who took a chance and got them a meeting.

Master Quoda agreed, and added, "First you identify and keep your champion close. Also, you may have more than one champion. At first it may be a new recruit like Ally, but as you go higher in the organization, you will want to add an advocate with buying power. Keep all of your allies close. Very close. Treat them well. Or a smart competitor will take your champion, and you will lose your sale."

Master Quoda further advised, "Your champion has both professional and personal goals that you need to learn. While helping you meet your goals, your champion will wonder,

'What's in it for me?' (WIIFM). Help further their goals, and your champion will continue to back your company. Treat your champion well, and you will both benefit from the alliance."

Luck and Solow realized, with some regret, that the least they could have done was to have taken Ally out to a nice lunch and interviewed her about the needs and goals of Stellar Corporation. They would have received information worth much more than the few dollars it cost them to buy her favorite Cobb salad.

Next, Master Quoda quizzed them on the financial decision maker at Stellar Corporation.

Luck and Solow had to admit that they didn't know the person who fulfilled that role. Now they knew what they needed to learn next. They made a note to talk to Ally, their champion, about who this person was at Stellar Corporation, and to ask her if she could provide them with an organization chart.

Quoda reminded them, "The same approach you use regarding your champion must be applied to the financial decision maker. You must make the decision maker enthusiastic to buy, and you must understand their buying process."

Master Quoda then stressed the importance of knowing the buying power of the company and the person who approves the purchasing. "Do they have the authority and the funds to buy the Life Star? You must understand the company, their purchasing policies and the purchasing chain of command. Do you know why?"

Luck quickly answered, "We can't get a sale from a person who doesn't have the power to say 'yes.'"

Master Quoda was pleased with his answer and it saved Luck a whack of knowledge to the head. He went on to detail the difference between the gatekeepers and the real decision makers.

"A gatekeeper may handle and sign purchasing paperwork. This person might be able to slow or accelerate the buying process, and in some cases, influence the decision makers. The decision makers may be an individual or a com-mittee. Your mission is to get to the highest decision maker. It is important to know all of the players involved, so you can use the right channels to get the sale. Do you know how to find out if your contact can make the final decision?"

The two looked dumbfounded.

"Remember, you also have two ears, and one mouth."

Still the two sat silently staring at Quoda.

"Just ask," said Master Quoda. "Ask how decisions of this size are made, who has the authority to make decisions of this type, and what the actual steps are in the process."

Solow grasped the issue at hand. "Master," he asked, "can our champion help us get a meeting with the decision maker?"

Master Quoda nodded. "Right you are."

"Then what?" asked Luck.

Master Quoda smiled and answered, "First, forget about luck. And forget about going solo. Those things might get you an appointment, but as you have already learned, they won't get you the sale. You only get one shot. And if you don't master the Sales Force, the competition will take your business."

Feeling nervous, Luck asked, "How do we not blow our presentation?" Solow added, "How do we impress the decision maker with only one shot?"

Again, Master Quoda offered his sage advice: "Solve your customer's problems."

"How is that possible?" asked Luck.

Master Quoda imparted this instruction: "Either on the phone or in person, it is all about 'talking problems.' Offering solutions comes later. In this way, your customer can understand the value of your product to their niche market challenges. Because you've been listening to their unique needs the entire time, you are in a position to show them that your product can take their company to the next level.

"Masters of the Sales Force help the buyer see that the problem is serious enough to justify making a change. Asking the right questions can help the customer identify problem areas and become more anxious for a solution that will take the pain of the problem away. And when they find the right solution in your product, they get recognition and become more valuable to their company."

Solow looked excited. "So by asking Stellar Corporation how reduced costs, how increased security, and how enhanced working conditions would impact their company, we are working toward making a sale?"

Master Quoda nodded. "Some of the questions you want to ask are?"

Luck and Solow started throwing out questions they wished they had asked:

- What is your vision for the business?
- How is your success measured?
- If you could wave a magic wand and make anything happen here, what would the solution look like?
- What happens if it is not completed?
- What is the cost to the business if it is not completed?
- What will the best (your product) do for your business?
- A problem this big must have been noticed before. How is it that nothing was done before now?

"Good, very good," said Master Quoda, "yet, that is not all. The next step is to remove all obstacles and red lights.

Done correctly, your sales presentation will be music to your customer's ears. This will help accelerate the decision-making process. To remove obstacles and red lights, you must have ready 'Plan B' solutions for your customer to address any objection.

"For example," he continued, "if Stellar Corporation has an objection about pricing, you are ready with pricing solutions that still move them forward. Ask if a 30-day trial, leasing options, payment plans, or a retainer to lock in the pricing and delivery date would be of assistance. Then listen..."

Master Quoda noticed Solow staring off into the night sky. He raised his cane ready to deliver another whack of knowledge.

Realizing what was coming, Solow quickly said, "But what if our price is too high?"

Master Quoda cleared his throat and continued. "As the customer evaluates your solution, listen and revisit what they are losing if they don't purchase the Life Star. You must learn their real objections before dropping your price."

Luck asked, "Master Quoda, if I know both the champion and the decision maker, will they tell me what the red lights are?"

"Wise you are, young student of the Sales Force. Yes, when you create a relationship that is a partnership, you will get all the information you need. 'Close a sale' it is not. 'Creating a partnership and delivering solutions,' it is."

Luck's and Solow's eyes glistened. They were beginning to think differently and see the power of the Sales Force. Even more importantly, not only did they understand why Stellar Corporation had said "No" to the Life Star, they were also beginning to understand how they could get them to say "Yes."

 **CHAPTER 8**

The Power of the Dark Side

AS LUCK would have it, after the daily lessons a call came in from a buyer in another galaxy who was rumored to have tons of cash. This buyer said his company was hot for the Life Star and wanted a meeting immediately.

Quoda warned Luck and Solow that they were not yet Masters of the Sales Force, and although the lure of the dollar was strong, they were still vulnerable, as they had not yet completed their training. But Luck and Solow had dollar signs in their eyes. The desire for a big commission blinded them, as it has so many business owners, on planets all across the universe.

They were so eager to sell the Life Star that all their Sales Force training went out the window. They skipped researching the buyer and finding out about the real decision maker. Luck and Solow were focused on one thing: The buyer had the cash to buy a hundred Life Stars and make them rich!

It was a breathy phone call from a certain Dark Dubious with the Dark Side Corporation that hooked them. He flattered Luck and Solow with compliments about their brilliant invention, and how the Stellar Corporation was full of imbeciles for not buying the Life Star immediately. Their loss was his gain, he explained. Gain they would as Luck and Solow were about to become the richest duo in the galaxy!

Dark Dubious arranged for a private luxury shuttle to take them away from the dreary swamp planet in one hour – and left instruction that they should not be late!

On the way to the dark planet, Luck and Solow sipped complimentary Dark Side champagne, confident that someone finally appreciated the Life Star. Getting their first mega-sale would be easier than they thought.

But after the first buzz of excitement wore off, Luck started to get nervous. He quickly did some research on the Dark Side Corporation in the shuttle, and what he uncovered gave him chills. Dark Side had horrible reviews all across the galaxy wide social web. Dubious was known to strangle employees if they failed him in any way. There were even hints of extortion and monopolistic threats reported in the news.

"I have a bad feeling about this," Luck whispered to Solow.

"Just go with it. I've got it covered," said Solow.

Luck and Solow landed on a dark planet far, far, away. Escorted by armor-suited security guards, they met Dark Dubious in his corner office overlooking the galaxy. In their sales presentation, Luck and Solow laid out exactly what the Life Star could do – its systems, specifications, and how it worked.

At first, Luck wondered to himself what he had been worried about. Dark Dubious was so…nice. He complemented Luck and Solow and poured them glass after glass of Dark Side champagne. He levitated pens. Luck and Solow were having a great time. Dubious spoke of the future, and what a long and lucrative relationship they would have with the Dark Side Corporation. He asked them to leave product blueprints behind for him to peruse. They gladly did. Everything seemed perfect until Dark Dubious heard everything he needed from Luck and Solow.

Abruptly, the tone of the meeting changed. Dubious ominously thanked Luck and Solow for a very eventful meeting and dismissed them with an "I'll think about it."

Not wanting to leave without the sale and betray their dreams of getting rich, Luck and Solow jumped in with an anemic attempt at using the Sales Force. Dark Dubious let loose an evil laugh.

Suddenly, their necks felt tight and they found it difficult to breathe. Security guards filled the room. The Emperor of

Dark Side, Inc. walked in and joined them, and Dark Dubious handed him Luck and Solow's blueprints for the Life Star.

"My Lord, I was successful in procuring the exact product specifications. With our sales team trained in dark side sales, our corporation can rule the galaxy!"

Luck and Solow were stunned. They wanted to kick themselves. Not only were they getting cut out of their own invention, Dark Dubious wasn't even a true decision maker! The Sales Force couldn't protect them because they had skipped Master Quoda's important first lesson: **Protect your product.** They had no Non-Disclosure Agreement (NDA), no trademark, no patent, nor a community to protect them. Legally, they were completely vulnerable to Dark Dubious' stealing the Life Star concept and manufacturing it on his own.

Immediately they also realized how important it was to establish a market presence. With a public website, a social media fan base, and publicity, they would be protected by having a core audience that could essentially help protect their ideas, concepts, products, and entire business.

Shaking off their regrets and content to escape with their lives, Luck and Solow commandeered a Dark Side shuttle and narrowly escaped while Dubious and the Emperor were disputing renaming the product "The Dark Star," "The Deadly Star," or...

They quickly flew back to the swamp planet, where

Quoda waited.

CHAPTER 9

Training Begins...Again

"HOLD ON," I say, "I've heard this part of the story before. But it was different..."

"Well, this is the real story," says the Bull. "Please, sit still and listen."

* * *

Luck and Solow were back to square one. At this point the two were at an all-time low. They realized that not following the steps of the Sales Force had cost them more than just a sale; it also threatened to cost them their reputation, one of the most difficult things to rebuild in the galaxy.

Luck asked Master Quoda why he had let them go when surely he knew what would happen at Dark Side Corporation.

Master Quoda replied, "Companies like Dark Side

Corporation are unethical; you have to protect yourselves legally from them. Even if you get a sale from them, they can run your company into the ground. They won't pay on time, they may undercut payments, and they may work you to the bone for impossible deliverables. That is not a client that you can afford to have."

Luck and Solow thoroughly understood how doing business with the wrong company could be disastrous.

"The same can be true for every company, to some extent. That is why it is up to you, young Masters of the Sales Force, to identify and eliminate all 'red lights' from the beginning. You see, getting closer to not just any sale, but to closing the right sale with win-win benefits, is the goal. Once a Master of the Sales Force, you will always know when to negotiate, and when to walk away."

Master Quoda paused, and then addressed their initial question: "Sometimes, you have to learn the Sales Force through failure before you are ready to really listen. And now you see exactly how following the steps of the Sales Force can solve one or more of your problems, so you are ready to do whatever it takes to become masters of it."

In a flash, Luck and Solow got it.

The Sales Force itself was about solving problems.

"Teach us from the beginning, Master Quoda," said Luck and Solow. "We will learn and adhere to its every step."

Master Quoda nodded, then motioned for RMG to project again the first lesson of the Sales Force into the dark night sky.

1. **CREATE A BEST SELLING PRODUCT**
   A. TEST THE MARKET
   B. PROPER FUNDING
   C. PROTECT YOUR ASSETS
   D. BUILD INCREDIBLE SALES TOOLS

Master Quoda explained, "It is blind excitement that makes one think that the galaxy will be as excited about our idea as we are. In the mind, ideas are perfect, full, and complete. But when we bring them out of our mind's eye and into the three-dimensional world there is always a learning curve. Things are not as we thought them to be. There are glitches, design flaws, market quirks and manufacturing problems that can sink your project if not properly thought out."

Solow asked, "Is there a way to prevent this?"

Again, Master Quoda was impressed with the question. He replied: "Yes, in fact that is one of the best uses of the Sales Force. Testing the market allows you to foresee many potential issues and find solutions for them before you are in too deep financially. You may find that the issues are too vast to make a profit and scrap the project before spending millions on something that will not have market potential.

"Masters of the Sales Force ask must ask themselves these questions: 'What is the need for our product in the marketplace? Will it help a large population solve a problem or meet a goal?' If it does, then continue. And if it does not, then you will likely not be successful in your business."

"We know our Life Star would have been a bestseller," said Luck. "If we had the chance..."

"Right you may be," said Master Quoda. "To effectively know your funding needs, you must build a product prototype.

Not only does this allow you to see any potential design flaws, it also gives incredible insight into production costs. You will get a feel for exactly how you must price your product to turn a profit and how much time it will take to cover your overhead expenses and have your company in the black. In this way, you will know what you can promise your future clients in terms of delivery."

Master Quoda continued. "When creating a prototype, Masters of the Sales Force must ask themselves these questions about their product: Is it scalable? Is it repeatable? Know you must, whether your solution is able to scale to target audience, what size the audience is, who they are, and who else would benefit. Do you have a plan in place, and resources at the ready? If so, you can grow your business without stopping and have an action plan in place.

"Once you have this information, you can calculate the amount needed for sufficient initial funding, as well for growth of your company."

Suddenly, Master Quoda's eyes turned down. Even RMG hung his head.

Was that...a tear?

Luck and Solow were concerned. "Is everything okay, Master Quoda?" asked Solow.

Master Quoda explained: "I have seen too many young students of the Sales Force fail by not giving themselves enough funding for their companies to turn a profit. They were forced out of business, even with the best prototypes, simply because they didn't allow themselves enough time as a startup business to be profitable. It's a big galaxy out there and we can travel at the speed of light. But it can take even the best product two or three years to generate income. And if you haven't given yourself enough funding, you won't make it."

Luck and Solow realized that they had made that mistake. They thought the Life Star would be an instant hit throughout the galaxy. It never crossed their minds that it might take years for the Life Star to gain enough traction in the market to turn a profit. They certainly didn't budget for that possibility.

"We are listening, Master Quoda," they assured him.

Master Quoda again was pleased and went on:

"Once you have found your place in the market, made a successful prototype, effectively priced your product, and found the funding to give yourselves the necessary time to turn a profit, the next step in the Sales Force is to protect your product. The better protected your product is, the more successful you will be. And that means you must anticipate future liabilities, ensure proper legal protection, hire the right team, and outpace strong competition."

Luck and Solow thought back to the very beginning when they turned up their noses at what they thought was "extra work." It seemed like so long ago when all they wanted to do was create a product, get excited, and let nature take its course. Now, they felt differently. They realized that the value in the Sales Force is how each step is an integral part of the whole. If they had only followed this step before meeting with the Dark Side Corporation, they would have had a protected concept and product. Rather than having the idea stolen, they would have launched with a marketing machine along with a protected product, and that would have made them extremely successful.

Luck and Solow knew that the Life Star wouldn't be their only invention. They already had other ideas taking shape in their minds. And next time would be different, because now they knew what to do. Next time would be faster, easier, and more profitable.

They reviewed Lessons 2 and 3 again:

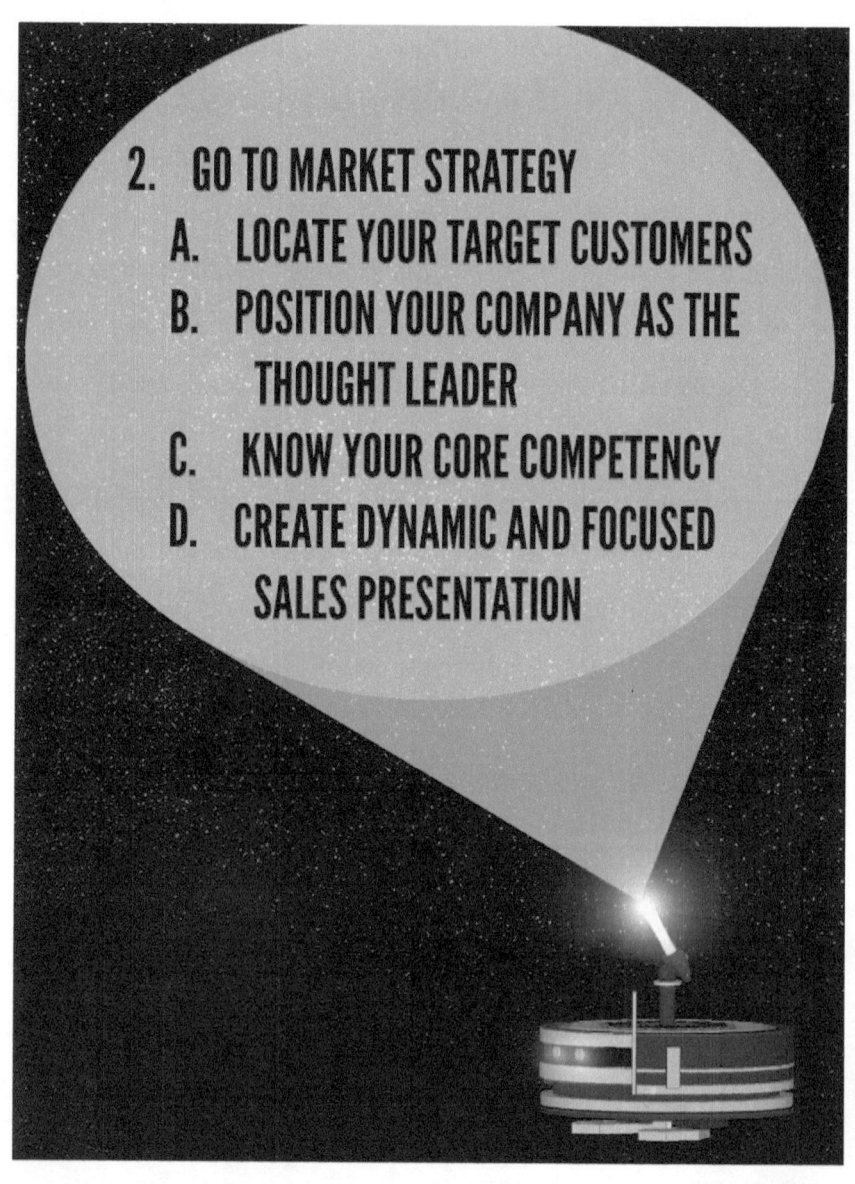

2. GO TO MARKET STRATEGY
   A. LOCATE YOUR TARGET CUSTOMERS
   B. POSITION YOUR COMPANY AS THE THOUGHT LEADER
   C. KNOW YOUR CORE COMPETENCY
   D. CREATE DYNAMIC AND FOCUSED SALES PRESENTATION

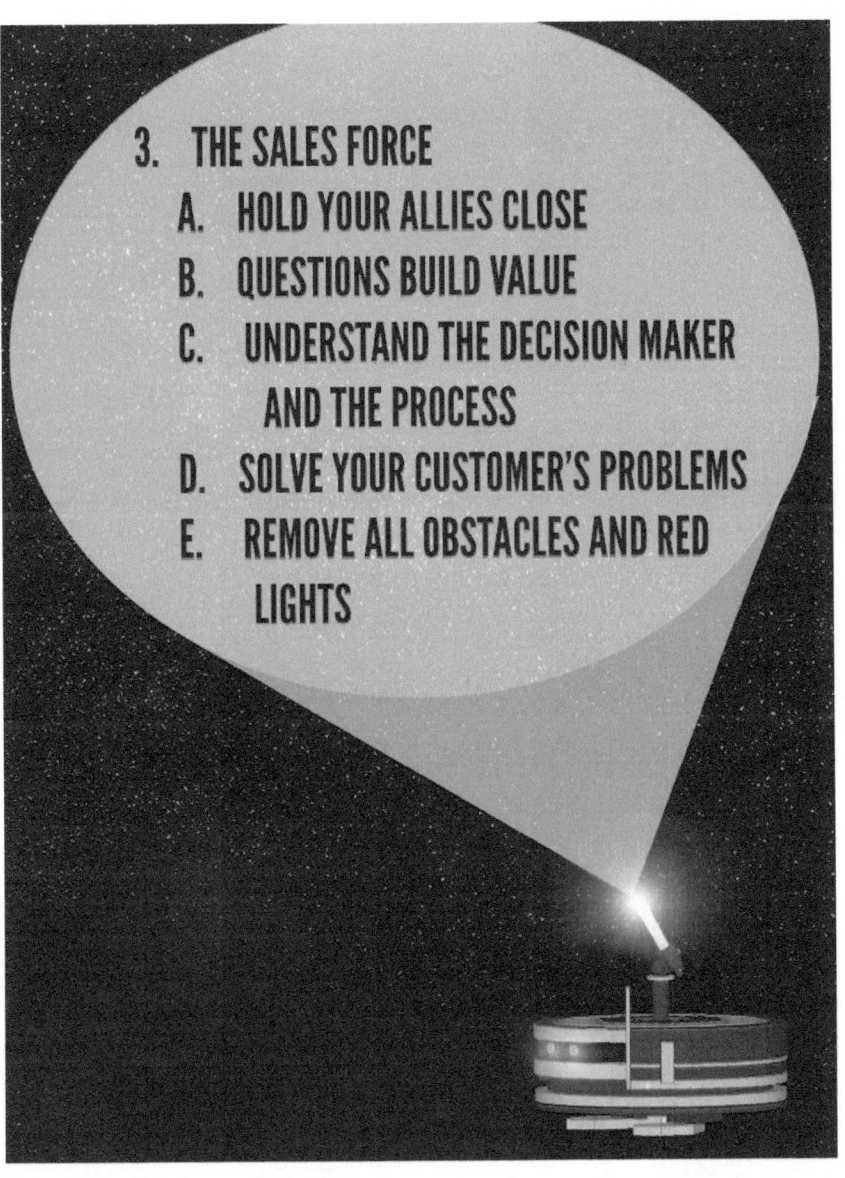

3. THE SALES FORCE
   A. HOLD YOUR ALLIES CLOSE
   B. QUESTIONS BUILD VALUE
   C. UNDERSTAND THE DECISION MAKER AND THE PROCESS
   D. SOLVE YOUR CUSTOMER'S PROBLEMS
   E. REMOVE ALL OBSTACLES AND RED LIGHTS

CHAPTER 10

Grow Your Business with the Sales Force

WITH THEIR NEW understanding of how the Sales Force could be repeated and refined for every new product Luck and Solow would bring to market, Master Quoda signaled for RMG to illuminate the final lesson of the Sales Force into the night sky.

"It is up to you to manage customer expectations and make deliverables reasonable," he explained. "Otherwise, even a top-earning account can bog down productivity and leave less time to prospect new accounts. By developing set processes and account management, you can ensure that you are continually being the solution to your clients' problems. That is why it is imperative to set appropriate customer expectations and satisfaction levels from the very beginning. You must systemize your communication with customers to relay the value of your product immediately, effectively, and continuously.

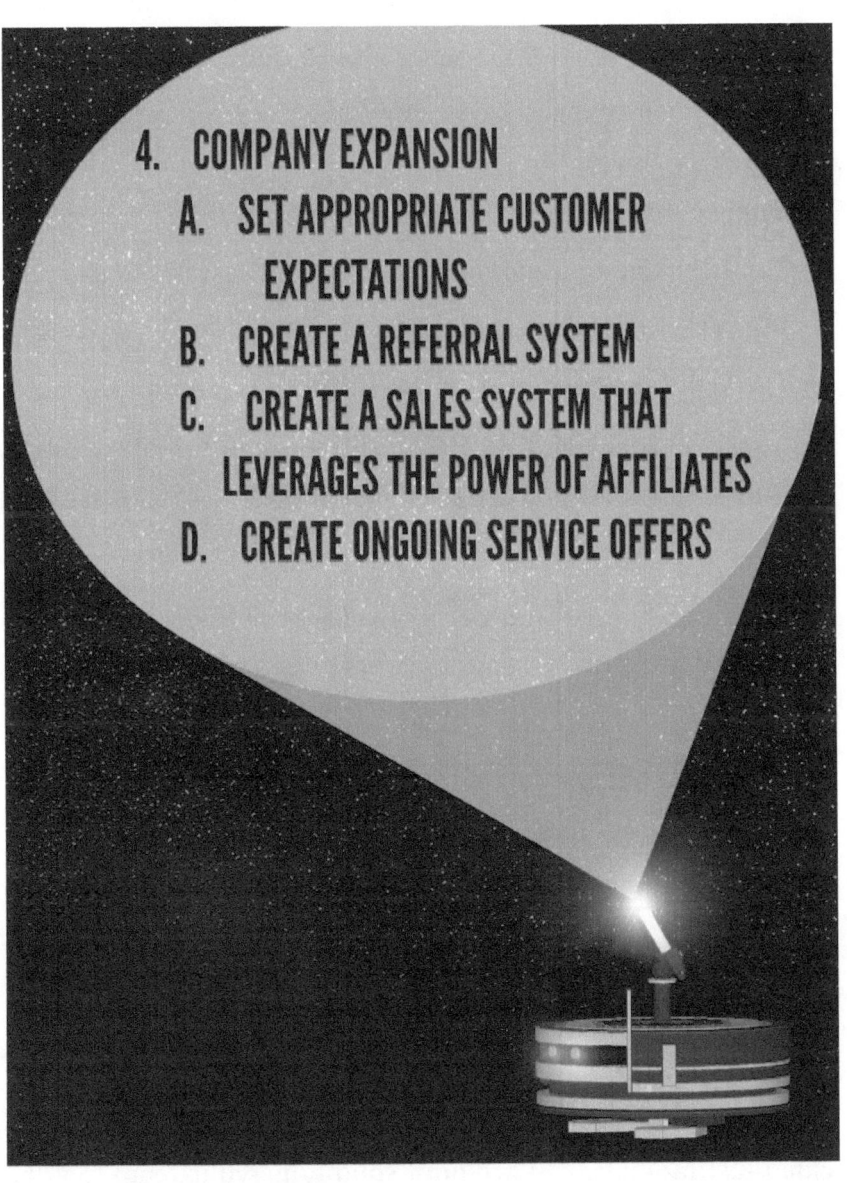

4. COMPANY EXPANSION
   A. SET APPROPRIATE CUSTOMER EXPECTATIONS
   B. CREATE A REFERRAL SYSTEM
   C. CREATE A SALES SYSTEM THAT LEVERAGES THE POWER OF AFFILIATES
   D. CREATE ONGOING SERVICE OFFERS

"To do this, first you want to evaluate your customer's current status. You can access this information by listening to what they are doing currently, so you can then solve their challenges. In turn, they can access how your product fulfills their needs better than what they are using, and how your product succeeds where their current system fails."

After taking a moment to consider Master Quoda's last point, Luck said, "If we follow these steps I see how we will succeed. But how do we grow our business?"

Master Quoda answered, "There are four ways to grow your business after you are established. The first is to set up a referral system. Satisfied customers are your best resources for new client referrals. If you arrange a lucrative referral system with your satisfied clients, they see the value in referring you, which is gold to both companies.

"In thanks, you must recognize the referral. You should create a thank you 'card' and send it immediately for each referral. Larger referrals may be worthy of more. Create a case study posted on your blog, and in your email newsletter, about how successful the company is. The larger the audience you have built on your social networks, the more powerful a complimentary article is. By going a step further and having video testimonials, you are both solidifying your team to keep a visible customer very happy, but also creating excellent social proof to your prospective client base, your current client base,

AND your customers client base. They will also send the videos out to improve their public standing.

"Sending a referral fee, discount, or donation to a charitable cause is also acceptable to say 'thank you.' Many referring clients just want to help. If they know you will deliver high value, they may feel confident in sending business to you without any fee in return.

"Never stop listening to your clients, because as their company grows so will their challenges. They will need different solutions. The more you are able to address their new challenges and offer a variety of solutions, the more loyal your customers will be.

"If you create solutions, you will be creating a sales system that multiplies with the power of VARs and affiliates."

"What are VARs and affiliates?" asked Luck.

Master Quoda smiled at the question, and observed Solow listening intently. "This is the second way to grow your business," he said. "VARs are 'value-added resellers.' Luck and Solow, you are just the power of two. Imagine having a sales force of hundreds, or even thousands, recommending and selling your product by crafting dedicated alliances within niche markets. Each niche will have resellers that use or adapt your product in conjunction with their products, and add value to the solution.

"Affiliates prospect for leads and create partners purely

for sales credit. With the proper affiliates, you will hit a tipping point in your business where growth will happen exponentially. Online affiliates often use advertising methods including organic search engine optimization, or SEO, paid search engine marketing, known as PPC or Pay Per Click, e-mail marketing, and in some cases, display advertising."

This hit home for Solow. Even though he thought Luck was amazing, and his dream was to operate independently with just the two of them, he knew they were limited. A sales team of thousands working under him would provide massive opportunities to expand their business. But he didn't know how to go about creating this kind of sales system.

Here, Master Quoda wisely advised them to ask for help from someone who was already a Master of the Sales Force. "Every entrepreneur has strengths and weaknesses. It is critical to work from your strengths, rather than spending large amounts of time trying to improve your weaknesses. Where there is weakness, find a person who is strong in that area, and add them to your team. They can easily do the work that you struggle with. They may teach you how to be a Master of that area as well."

Master Quoda went on to the third way to grow business: "to create ongoing service offerings out of the growing needs of your customers. This creates multiple income streams that can be adding revenue daily, weekly, monthly, quarterly, or yearly. This is important to growing a business, because you can anticipate your income and make projections based on that information. When you aren't dependent solely on getting new clients and are servicing those that you already have, you create consistent income."

Now Luck and Solow's heads were really spinning. They could envision not only the business of their primary product, but also service products, maintenance products, white label products, and much more. Suddenly, they could see that the Life Star they had invented was not just a single product, but rather, a brand. If only they hadn't skipped the first step of the Sales Force and had protected the Life Star. Next time, they promised themselves, would be different.

Master Quoda continued, "The fourth way to continue growing your business is through the smart use of social networking, such as the Galactic Wide Web and social media sites, like 'Spacebook,' which is quite a favorite in the galaxy.

"It is imperative to be easily found on the Web when customers are searching for something you may offer. With proper demonstrations of value, as well as giving expertise on information via regular updates to your website, you will attract both customers and complimentary affiliate partners. In this way, your business site will move up in relevance and appear immediately when a search related to your product is conducted. Every time there is a positive conversation about your business and your brand, you will improve your visibility in the Web marketplace."

Master Quoda asked RMG to look up Luck and Solow's website. RMG displayed the site and showed, through available free plug-ins, that the duo had no Search Engine Optimization on their site to attract buyers. He displayed the use of Galactic-Flash the Cheapwebba.com web designer used. Effectively, RMG demonstrated that their website was invisible to most popular phones and tablets in the galaxy.

Next, RMG showed how the duo had not even purchased their own names at a .com registrar. In fact, Solow's full name was purchased, and owned, by the Dark Side Corporation, who was directing all searches for Solow's name to the Dark Side product page.

Solow was shocked. His very name was owned by someone else. Luck was excited: "You mean that if we had this information when we started, our website would have attracted our target market, our opening video would have explained our core competency, and by just having testimonials, clients and partners would want to work with us – 24/7?"

"Yes...and so much more," said Master Quoda.

"Maybe the partners would even want to create more complete product offerings for our clients, just by having the right galactic website built?"

"Yes, but..."

Luck and Solow both chimed in: "It's all based upon listening to market needs."

Master Quoda and RMG exchanged a knowing glance: Luck and Solow had successfully learned the Sales Force.

Chapter 11

Getting the Sale

LUCK AND SOLOW were eager to get back home immediately and start applying the lessons of the Sales Force to their new idea: The Aura Wand 3000. But Solow had a realization. They were young masters of the Sales Force. He observed it would be wise for them to hire someone much more experienced to expertly guide them through the process.

Master Quoda again was pleased. "You have learned well, young masters of the Sales Force. Time is money. It is more costly to learn from your own mistakes than to pay someone with expertise honed though years of experience."

"Are you available for the next week?" Solow asked.

Over the next few days, Luck and Solow worked side by side with Master Quoda on each of the steps of the Sales Force creating the Aura Wand 3000. Before they knew it, they were ready to present to Stellar Corporation.

This time, Luck and Solow's website was 'Web 2.0,'

branded consistently with integrated explanation and promotional videos. The site had endorsements, a press release was issued, and a stellar sales presentation was all ready to complement the prototype product.

This was the correct way to launch their brand, and they were proud.

Luck and Solow met Ally, their champion, and showed off their exceptional two-sentence elevator pitch detailing exactly what their new Aura Wand 3000 could do to benefit Stellar Corporation against the Dark Side. This was, of course, at her favorite restaurant.

Ally immediately saw the benefits of the Wand 3000 and was clear on how it would solve Stellar Corporation's growing problems. And with Master Quoda's powerful endorsement, Ally had no qualms about immediately setting up a sales meeting with Stellar Corporation. Not to mention, Master Quoda, another champion, had insider knowledge of the real decision maker in charge of purchasing at Stellar Corporation. With that information, Luck and Solow were able to negotiate a one-on-one meeting with the decision maker, rather than with the general Stellar committee.

This time, Luck and Solow were ready. This time it felt much different. They had a strong brand, and were confident and prepared. They felt powerful because they were using the Sales Force. While working with Master Quoda, Luck and

Solow had listened to the needs of the Stellar Corporation. They had intel that the Dark Side had just upgraded their competitive light swords, which put the entire galaxy at a disadvantage. Stellar Corporation needed a solution. And they needed it now.

It was Luck and Solow's job in the sales presentation to show exactly how they had the solution to the problem by visually presenting the value of their product. They had a gorgeous video hologram explaining the details of how the product would work for the Stellars. They displayed the **DREAM** of having solved the problem, the **PAIN** of not having it, and what the **SOLUTION** would do for them.

They also proposed, via a storyboard, a series of training videos that could be viewed by every user of the product. This benefited the Stellar Corporation, and Luck and Solow as well. Both companies would have fewer questions about how to use the new Aura Wand 3000, saving time and money.

Luck and Solow got the sale.

Stellar Corporation ordered 4,500 new Aura Wands. But Luck and Solow didn't stop there. They prospected within the account to see where Stellar Corporation could benefit from their expertise as consultants, and landed two related divisions soon after.

With Master Quoda's expert coaching, Luck and Solow continued to expand. They sold Stellar Corporation the Aura Wand servicing package with a hologram-emitting video microchip. It would deliver new techniques, moves, and unique uses of the Wands to the Stellars every month, which created consistent income that they could count on quarterly.

Luck and Solow anticipated that Stellar Corporation would be referring them to other galactic companies as well, so they structured a lucrative referral plan to accelerate the process. They co-branded a website landing page highlighting both companies' offerings, custom tailored for each industry they targeted.

Indeed, the referrals began flooding in for not only their Aura Wand 3000 but also all the ancillary packages they created under Master Quoda's tutelage.

Luck and Solow's dream came true. They went on to become two of the most successful business owners in the galaxy. Using the power of the Sales Force, they made millions in sales and rolled out new products twice a year that were well received across the galaxy.

Often they went back to Master Quoda for a whack of knowledge of the Sales Force, for there was always something more to learn in the advanced Sales Force training. Luck and Solow also kept Master Quoda on as a consultant for their company. Only this time, they didn't travel to the humid swamp planet. Instead, they sent a private shuttle to bring Master Quoda to them with complimentary Luck & Solow Corporation champagne.

Chapter 12

Lessons Learned

THE BULL LEANS BACK in his office chair, totally relaxed with his feet up on the desk. I sit with my eyes wide open, suddenly noticing just how big his ears are. And is that a cane next to his desk?

"What happened next?" I ask, not knowing if I have been sitting in his office for an hour or ten.

"It's simple. Luck and Solow used the Sales Force for every new product they launched and sold. They used video and internet marketing to be the tireless sales team that generates more revenue than they dreamed. Eventually, they also hired sales teams that grew to one hundred people in just two years, to support the thousands of online affiliates referring business to them, because they used the Sales Force effectively. As you can see, there comes a time in every company when only masters of the Sales Force can stay, and the under-performers have to go."

Just like Luck and Solow, I learned to listen.

I reflect on these lessons. I see how *everyone*, in every phase of business, can use these lessons and effectively grow business. Fantastic. The time to put these lessons to good use is right now.

"Bull, I have an account wavering on a decision to buy, and it has been months. This account alone would double my sales and would secure my job."

"Let's talk it though," says The Bull.

"It looks like I am stuck in Lesson 3: The Sales Force. Right?"

Bull looks at his cane like he might give me a whack of knowledge. "Did you cover all of Lesson 3's steps?"

That's when I summarize the steps in Lesson 3 for him in one word: QUODA. As in:

> **Q**uestions: Be prepared to ask excellent questions, not just do a presentation.
>
> **U**nderstanding: Current situation, goals, and what problems our solution solves.
>
> **O**bstacles: How do I locate and remove the red lights?
>
> **D**ecision-Making Process: Who is the decision maker?
>
> **A**dvocate: Who are my allies, and when they ask, "What's in it for me?" (WIIFM) what do I offer?

The Bull looks a bit stunned, yet happy. "Excellent. Even I hadn't seen that before. Sounds like a perfect time to take your champion to lunch. If you do follow QUODA and know the personal win, what the decision-making process is, who touches the paperwork, and what the financial decision maker wants, you won't be waiting for years. You'll deliver exactly what they want. Let me know how it goes."

Less than a week later, I learn all I need, and so much more, from my champion. With the new information, the client wants to move forward with us as much as we want to with them.

This assures my job is more than secure. In fact, I am now on top of the list, next to Bull.

I take him to lunch. I detail how I spoke with my champion and was able to home in on exactly what the issue was.

"The company was having delivery issues and they knew the exact cost to the business. I asked her to take me through the actual decision-making process including who needed to sign off on this project to get it over the line. And she literally walked me through their building, introducing me to each of the people who touch the contract. I gave each of them a quick reminder of proven benefits, and a list of testimonials we had recorded from our other clients.

"After viewing our website which supported what I explained, she told me that the CFO wanted to lease as it was better for their taxes than an outright purchase.

"It was so simple, Bull," I say, "I called our new V.P., Don D'Man, who could approve a three-year lease, and he did. Problem solved!"

The Bull nods. "He just wants success. He will help any way he can and needs people that can grow our business. People who have a scalable and repeatable system."

"I realize that I used to be operating solely on long days and luck, rather than a system that can be repeated, client after client. D'Man mentioned he would bring me along on his next million-dollar start-up adventure, as this is the kind of sales system that he needs to use to grow business. Your story changed everything."

"Congratulations, you are about to make a million in sales. Do you know why?" asks Bull.

"Because I am able to show my clients how to solve their problems."

A smile spreads across Bull's face. "You made it. Welcome to success."

"Thank you."

"Oh, one last thing..."

"What's that?" I ask.

"May The Sales Force Be With You."

Appendix A

The Sales Force: The Four Lessons

1. **Create an Incredible Product**
    a. *Test the Market*
    b. *Proper Funding*
    c. *Protect your Assets*
    d. *Build Incredible Sales Tools*
2. **Go To Market Strategy**
    a. *Locate Your Target Customers*
    b. *Position Your Company as the Thought Leader*
    c. *Know Your Core Competency*
    d. *Create Dynamic and Focused Sales Presentation*
3. **The Sales Force**
    a. *Hold Your Allies Close*
    b. *Questions Build Value*
    c. *Understand the Decision Maker and the Process*
    d. *Solve Your Customer's Problems*
    e. *Remove All Obstacles and Red Lights*
4. **Company Expansion**
    a. *Set Appropriate Customer Expectations*
    b. *Create a Referral System*
    c. *Create a Sales System that Leverages the Power of Affiliates*
    d. *Create Ongoing Service Offers*

Appendix B

Q.U.O.D.A.

- Questions
    - (Be prepared to ask excellent questions, not just do a presentation.)
- Understanding
    - (Current situation, goals, and what does the solution solve?)
- Obstacles
    - (How do I locate and remove the red lights?)
- Decision Making Process
    - (Who is the decision maker?)
- Advocate
    - (Who are my allies or champions, and what is in it for them?)

Appendix C

Web Resources

For do-it-yourself website, blog, and press release sites to start building an audience you can use WordPress (wordpress.com), Twitter (www.twitter.com), Blogger (www.blogger.com), Tumblr (www.tumblr.com), Facebook (www.facebook.com), LinkedIn (www.linkedin.com), and Pinterest (www.pinterest.com).

There are many ways to generate traffic with press releases via www.vocus.com, and creating excellent blog content, as well as video content on YouTube (www.youtube.com), Vimeo (www.vimeo.com), and many others.

Measuring site traffic and analytics as well as SEO are critical as well (adwords.google.com; ads.youtube.com/keyword_tool).

Qualified specialists can help. More information and consultation to help guide you are available at www.ripmediagroup.com and www.salesforce.co.

Business search contacts and are stored in database websites that are available for fees at: www.hoovers.com, www.insideview.com, www.data.com, www.salesforce.com, www.linkedin.com, and many others.

More information on solutions like these can be found with consultants at:

http://ripmediagroup.com/businessbrief

About the Author

Maury F. Rogow has 20 years of successful experience in sales, marketing and business development. He began his career in the AT&T corporate development program, then with Lucent Technologies he dramatically increased market share for multimedia services and software through innovative sales campaigns.

He was recognized in the top 1% of Lucent's global sales force, and was awarded a coveted "Council of Leaders" title. Maury later joined a startup, which tripled its revenue and was successfully sold to Cisco Systems for over $1 billion. As Global Client Manager for Avaya, his efforts earned him the "Leadership Award in Global Sales and Marketing" for generating millions in new revenue streams.

He started his own firm to produce marketing media and help others achieve success in business. Currently working with multiple brands expanding their markets, the company donates a portion of proceeds to non-profit organizations and various charitable organizations.

Maury is Executive Producer of the feature film *Bedrooms*, as seen on Showtime, Co-Producer of feature film *SNAP*, Consulting Producer at CIMA Productions (Producer of Sundance Award Selection: Filly Brown), New Media Producer at Cabin 14 Productions, Producer of *The Shambler* and producer of hundreds of hours of branded commercials and animated videos. Maury received his BA from and an Executive MBA Certification in Global Technology from Tufts University/Lucent Technologies.

ADVANCED SALES FORCE TRAINING

I. Create an Incredible Product
    A. Test the Market
        1. List building
        2. Landing pages
    B. Proper Funding
    C. Protect your Assets
    D. Build Incredible Sales Tools
        1. Branding and logo
        2. Audio and video
        3. A Website That Sells
            a. Pictures
            b. Video Explanation
            c. Testimonials
            d. Dynamic website
            e. Winning sales copy
            f. Case studies
            g. Up sells – automate and expand margins
            h. Pictures of products
            i. Search Engine Optimization (SEO)
            j. Analytics / Measure
            k. Website Customer Tracking
        4. Product Launch - Automate
            a. Affiliates
            b. Webinars
            c. Awards
            d. Live events
            e. Post event follow up

II. Go To Market Strategy
    A. Locate Your Target Customers
    B. Position your Company as the thought Leader
    C. Friends, fans, followers build to each of the following
        1. Social media
        2. Blogs
        3. Newsletter
        4. Forum
        5. Automated webinars
        6. Know your core competency

7. Traffic generation
8. Online
    a. PPC
    b. Email
    c. SEO
    d. Viral Videos
    e. Social Media
9. Offline
    a. Radio
    b. Billboard
    c. Taxi, bus ads
    d. Trade journals
    e. Trade shows
    f. Public Speaking
    g. Networking events
    h. Conferences
    i. Partnerships
    j. Affiliates
10. Create dynamic and focused sales presentation

III. The Sales Force
  A. Hold Your Allies Close
  B. Questions build value
  C. Understand the Decision Maker and the Process
  D. Solve Your Customer's Problems
  E. Remove All Obstacles and Red Lights

IV. Company Expansion
  A. Set Appropriate Customer Expectations
  B. Create a Referral System
  C. Create a Sales System that Leverages the Power of Affiliates
  D. Partnerships
  E. Reseller pricing
  F. Referral fees
  G. Certifications
  H. Multiple engagement points –
    1. Slides
    2. Video
    3. Audio
  I. Create Ongoing Service Offers

YES, I WOULD LIKE TO GET STARTED!

AUTHOR IS AVAILABLE FOR HIRE ON THESE PRINCIPLES IN THIS BOOK

Please have a Sales Force representative contact me by phone or email for a risk-free consultation. I would also like to be registered for a monthly webinar and newsletter on the techniques taught in this book. I am under no obligation to buy anything and my contact information will be held in the strictest confidence.

Key frustrations:

1. Not enough leads/clients
2. No idea how to use Social Media or Video...even now
3. Need videos that sell
4. Business depends too much on one person
5. Expanding too fast to keep up
6. Need a good website, social media, and video marketing

You can fill out this form at:

ripmediagroup.com/businessbrief or
www.Ripmediagroup.com/salesforce

Or call: 888.899.8910

Start increasing your business by using Sales Force marketing today.